Dwarf Planets

Pluto, Charon, Ceres, and Eris

by Nancy Loewen   illustrated by Jeff Yesh

PICTURE WINDOW BOOKS
Minneapolis, Minnesota

Thanks to our advisers for their expertise, research, and advice:

Lynne Hillenbrand, Ph.D., Professor of Astronomy
California Institute of Technology

Terry Flaherty, Ph.D., Professor of English
Minnesota State University, Mankato

Editor: Jill Kalz
Designers: Amy Muehlenhardt and Angela Kilmer
Page Production: Melissa Kes
Art Director: Nathan Gassman
Associate Managing Editor: Christianne Jones
The illustrations in this book were created digitally.

Picture Window Books
5115 Excelsior Boulevard
Suite 232
Minneapolis, MN 55416
877-845-8392
www.picturewindowbooks.com

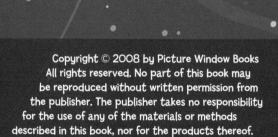

Printed in the United States of America.

All books published by Picture Window Books
are manufactured with paper containing at least
10 percent post-consumer waste.

Library of Congress Cataloging-in-Publication Data
Loewen, Nancy, 1964-
Dwarf planets : Pluto, Charon, Ceres, and Eris / by Nancy Loewen ;
illustrated by Jeff Yesh.
p. cm.
Includes index.
ISBN: 978-1-4048-3950-2 (library binding)
ISBN: 978-1-4048-3959-5 (paperback)
1. Dwarf planets—Juvenile literature. I. Yesh, Jeff, 1971- ill. II. Title.
QB698.L64 2008
523.4—dc22   2007032879

Table of Contents

Learning About Space

We learn something new about space every day.

Today, spacecraft travel millions of miles from Earth. They send back information about planets, moons, and other bodies in space. Telescopes put pictures of these faraway objects right before our eyes. Computers help scientists keep track of the reports that come in every day.

What Is a Major Planet?

A short time ago, scientists found a number of planet-like bodies at the edges of our solar system. They decided that a new definition of a planet was needed. Without one, the solar system might end up with thousands of planets!

A new definition was written in 2006. It said:

- A major planet is a body that orbits the sun (or another star).

- It must be round.

- It must have cleared all objects, such as other planets and asteroids, out of its path.

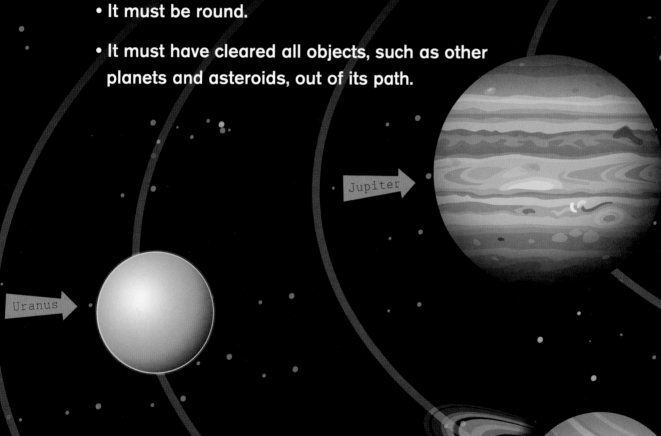

Jupiter

Uranus

Neptune

Saturn

FUN FACT
Scientists once said our solar system had nine planets:
Mercury, Venus, Earth, Mars, Jupiter, Saturn, Uranus,
Neptune, and Pluto. In 2006, scientists decided Pluto
should no longer be called a major planet.

EDITOR'S NOTE
In this illustration, the distances between planets
are not to scale. In reality, the distances between
the outer planets are much greater than the
distances between the inner planets.

The Dwarf Planets

Scientists also created a new group called "dwarf planets." Like a planet, a dwarf planet circles around the sun. It has a round shape. But it hasn't "cleared the neighborhood" around its orbit.

Pluto used to be listed as the smallest and farthest planet from the sun. It is now called a dwarf planet. Because of Pluto's small size, its gravity isn't strong enough to push other objects out of its path.

Scientists named three other dwarf planets as well. They are called Ceres, Charon, and Eris. The list of dwarf planets is likely to grow as more of the outer solar system is explored.

Pluto: A Lucky Find

Pluto was discovered in 1930. At that time, scientists were looking for an unknown planet. They believed that it was pushing Neptune onto a different path. Their data led them to Pluto.

Scientists were thrilled to discover Pluto. But they soon realized that Pluto was too small to sway Neptune. The search for "Planet X," a planet capable of pushing Neptune, continued for years.

Finally, in 1989, scientists gained a better understanding of Neptune's orbit from studying the motions of spacecraft sent to the outer solar system. They no longer believed there was a "Planet X."

FUN FACT
Pluto's orbit overlaps with that of Neptune. That's one of the reasons Pluto is a dwarf planet. For part of its orbit, Pluto is actually closer to the sun than Neptune is.

Far from the Sun

Pluto is more than 3.5 billion miles (5.6 billion kilometers) away from the sun. It lies in a far-off region of the solar system, beyond Neptune. The region includes thousands of icy, rocky bodies. Pluto, too, is made of rock and ice. Its diameter is less than one-fifth the diameter of Earth.

A Long, Cold Day and Year

Pluto spins slowly on its axis. A day is the amount of time a planet takes to spin on its axis one time. On Pluto, a day lasts nearly 154 Earth hours!

A year is the amount of time a planet takes to orbit once around the sun. One year on Pluto takes 248 Earth years.

Temperatures at Pluto's surface are thought to be minus 365 degrees Fahrenheit (minus 221 degrees Celsius). That makes Pluto one of the coldest objects in the solar system.

°F   °C

-365   -221

FUN FACT
In Roman mythology, Pluto was the god of the underworld. The Greeks called this god Hades.

Charon: A Double Dwarf Planet

Pluto has three moons. Two of them are tiny. They are called Nix and Hydra.

The other moon is called Charon. It is much larger than the others. Charon and Pluto circle around each other, locked together by gravity. They always keep the same face, or side, toward the other. Some scientists call Pluto and Charon "double dwarf planets."

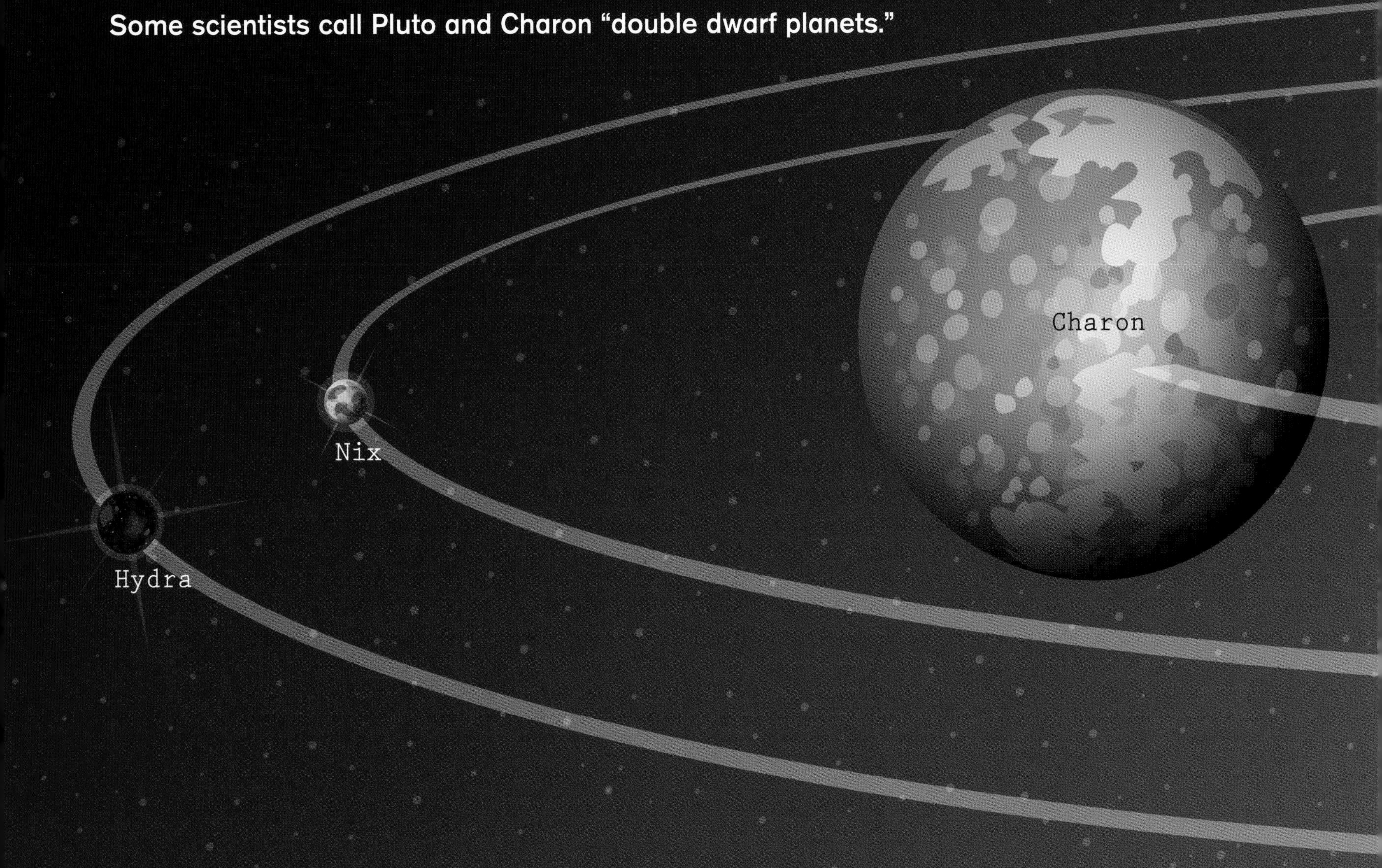

Charon

Nix

Hydra

FUN FACT
In Greek mythology, Charon was a ferryman (a person who carries passengers across water in a boat). He brought the souls of the dead to the underworld.

Ceres: No Longer Just an Asteroid

Ceres was discovered in 1801. It was the first object to be discovered in the asteroid belt. This region lies between Mars and Jupiter.

There are millions of asteroids in the asteroid belt. Most of them are probably less than a mile wide and appear in many odd shapes.

Jupiter

Ceres is different. It has a round shape. It's big. In 2006, scientists decided to call it a dwarf planet.

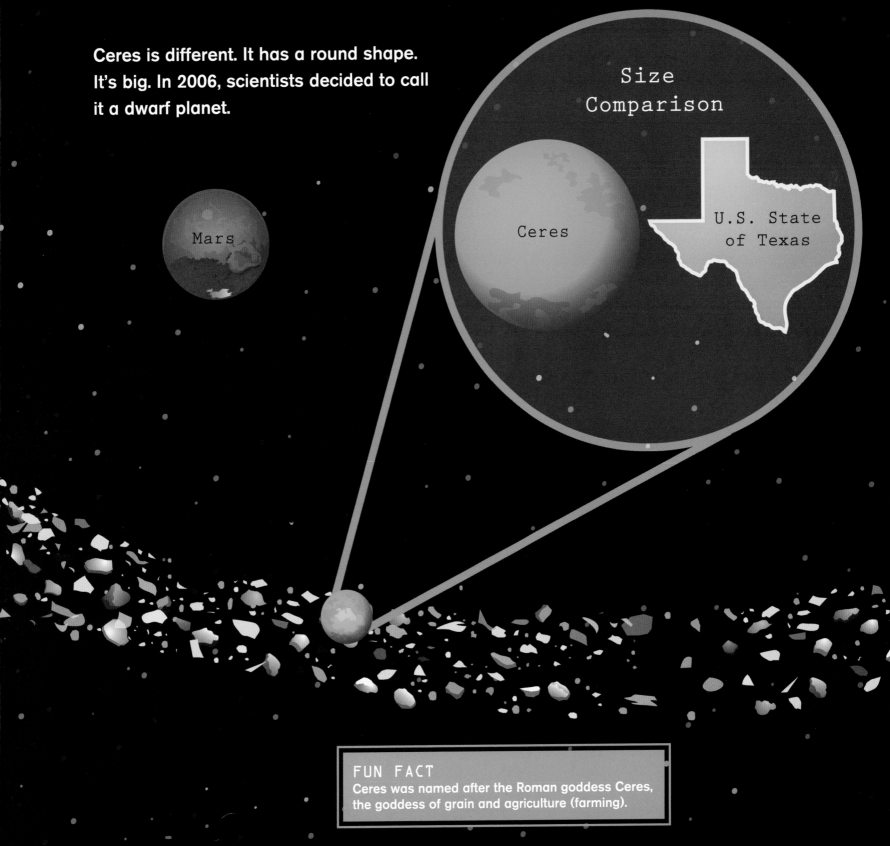

Mars

Size Comparison

Ceres

U.S. State of Texas

FUN FACT
Ceres was named after the Roman goddess Ceres, the goddess of grain and agriculture (farming).

Eris: The Largest Dwarf Planet

Found in 2005, Eris is the most recently discovered dwarf planet. It is also the most distant object found so far in the solar system. At the farthest point in its orbit, it is almost 10 billion miles (16 billion km) away from the sun. It takes Eris 557 Earth years to complete its orbit.

Eris is just a little larger than Pluto. It is the largest of the dwarf planets. It has at least one small moon, called Dysnomia.

Pluto, Charon, Ceres, and Eris are the first objects to be called dwarf planets. But many other bodies may someday be put into that group. Keep reading the news!

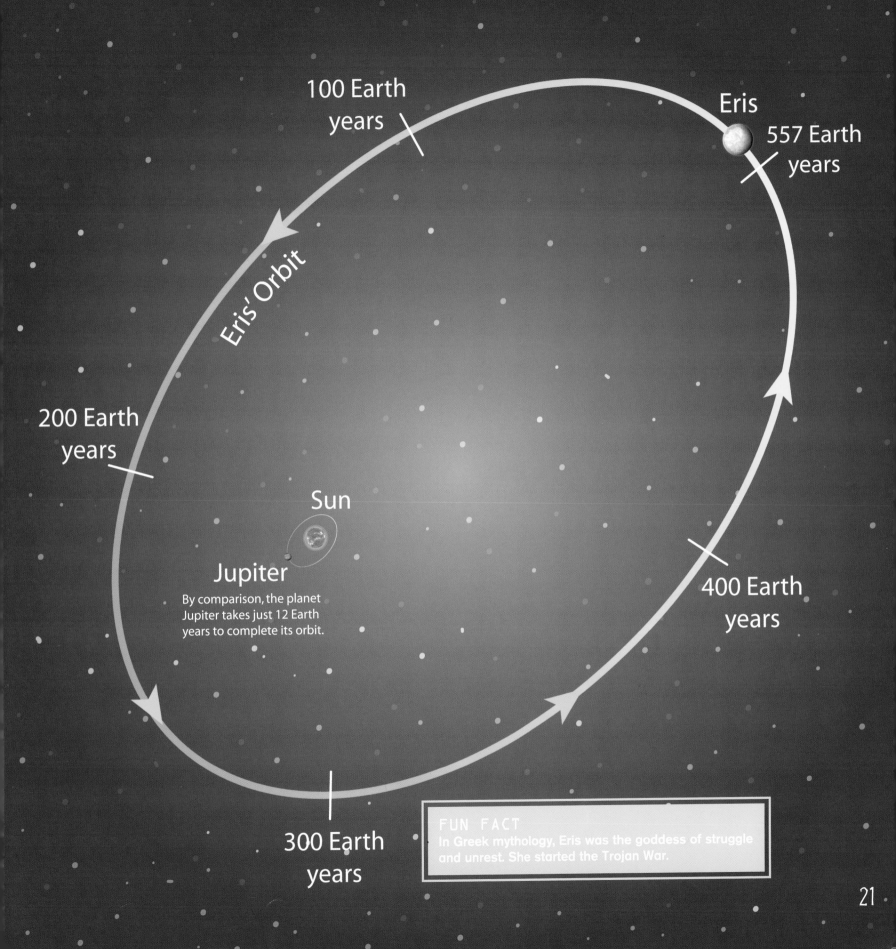

100 Earth years

Eris

557 Earth years

Eris' Orbit

200 Earth years

Sun

Jupiter

By comparison, the planet Jupiter takes just 12 Earth years to complete its orbit.

400 Earth years

300 Earth years

FUN FACT
In Greek mythology, Eris was the goddess of struggle and unrest. She started the Trojan War.

Memory Boosters

Here's a way to help you remember the order of things in a series, like the planets. Take the first letter of each item in the series. Then, make up a sentence, with each word starting with the letters, in order. Lots of kids remember the order of the planets this way. Here's an example:

My Very Excellent Mother Just Sent Us Nine Pizzas.

(Mercury, Venus, Earth, Mars, Jupiter, Saturn, Uranus, Neptune, Pluto)

But wait! Pluto is no longer called a planet. There can't be any pizzas now!

Make up your own sentence using eight words. The first letter for each word should match the order of the planets, ending with "N" (for Neptune). Get together with your friends, and write a bunch of them. Vote on the best one, and tell it to your classmates at school. Maybe it will spread all over the country!

You can also make up sentences for the dwarf planets. In order from the sun, they are Ceres, Charon, Pluto, and Eris. How about Certain Chickens Produce Eggs? Make your sentences as silly as you want—they'll still help you remember the serious stuff!

Fun Facts

- Pluto is smaller than seven moons in the solar system, including Earth's moon.

- A U.S. spacecraft called *New Horizons* was launched in January 2006. It will approach Pluto and Charon in 2015.

- At first, Ceres was thought to be a comet (an icy ball that orbits the sun). Then, for more than 150 years, it was thought to be an asteroid.

- In 2007, a spacecraft called *Dawn* was launched on a mission to study Ceres.

- While waiting for Eris to be officially named, some scientists gave it a nickname. They called it Xena, from the TV show "Xena: Warrior Princess." Eris' moon was nicknamed Gabrielle, Xena's sidekick on the show.

Glossary

asteroid—a rock that circles around the sun

atmosphere—the gases that surround a planet

axis—the center on which something spins, or rotates

diameter—the distance of a line running from one side of a circle, through the center, and across to the other side

gravity—the force that pulls things down toward the surface of a planet

orbit—the path an object takes to travel around a star or planet; also, to travel around a star or planet

solar system—the sun and the bodies that orbit around it; these bodies include planets, dwarf planets, asteroids, and comets

telescope—a device with mirrors or lenses; a telescope makes faraway objects appear closer

To Learn More

More Books to Read

Kortenkamp, Steve. *Why Isn't Pluto a Planet? A Book About Planets.* Mankato, Minn.: Capstone Press, 2007.

Landau, Elaine. *Pluto: From Planet to Ice Dwarf.* New York: Children's Press, 2007.

Orme, Helen, and David. *Let's Explore Pluto and Beyond.* Milwaukee: Gareth Stevens Pub., 2007.

On the Web

FactHound offers a safe, fun way to find Web sites related to topics in this book. All of the sites on FactHound have been researched by our staff.

1. Visit *www.facthound.com*
2. Type in this special code: 140483950X
3. Click on the FETCH IT button.

Your trusty FactHound will fetch the best sites for you!

Index

Look for all of the books in the Amazing Science: Planets series:

Brightest in the Sky: The Planet Venus
Dwarf Planets: Pluto, Charon, Ceres, and Eris
Farthest from the Sun: The Planet Neptune
The Largest Planet: Jupiter
Nearest to the Sun: The Planet Mercury
Our Home Planet: Earth
Ringed Giant: The Planet Saturn
Seeing Red: The Planet Mars
The Sideways Planet: Uranus